INTO THE ORANGE GROVE

INTO THE ORANGE GROVE

A COLLECTION OF POETRY

To Jackle, thank you for supporting me & my book!

Wander the grove...

BY GRACE HASSON

Grace Hasson

NEW DEGREE PRESS

INTO THE ORANGE GROVE
A Collection of Poetry

ISBN   978-1-64137-933-5 *Paperback*
        978-1-64137-730-0 *Kindle Ebook*
        978-1-64137-731-7 *Ebook*

To Dad, Mom and Aunt Joy, for your endless support.

To Annie and Ray, for reading every poem.

To Willow, for being the roots I stand on.

CONTENTS

NOTE FROM THE AUTHOR

*"To live and find out who you are, it's a quest, not a question.
. . .What I'm hungry for, what I've always been hungry for: a
way of seeing beyond the illusion of our separateness, into a
kind of togetherness that we all share all the time anyway."*

—DAVID KEPLINGER

The gentle snip of the scissors. The breath of water sprayed
onto moss. I used to watch my Dad trim his bonsai trees.
His tenderness looking out for such a small, living thing was
inspiring. Now, it reminds me of my journey making this
collection: the time spent deciding its shape and how much
to trim my words, along with letting my writing find a life of
its own. Some pieces needed major cutting back and others
needed room to grow.

Poems are like paintings; they capture one idea that can be
expanded and deepened but only if we look a little longer.
Sometimes the longer we look, the more we see ourselves and
our own experiences. Writing confessional poetry opened
me to seeing myself honestly. There was a time in my life
where I thought isolation was the answer. But after getting
help and reaching out to the people around me, I learned that
human connection is one of the most worthwhile, beautiful
things in life. I now share my poetry as a way to express and
to connect. I do this in the hopes that it will help people see
how being open might be transformative.

I imagine the moment I begin writing a poem: a sapling of connection peeks out of the soil. Each leaf is like a wave caught mid-crash, growing and spreading its green. This collection is a reflection of my mind and experiences. It takes you, as the title suggests, into my inner orange grove. In it I write about the way the people who have walked through my life have changed it and the way I have walked it. Though many of the poems deal with loneliness and being unarmed in a knife-fight against myself, the overall message is how I've grown from that. I've discovered poetry is a way to find the togetherness that poets like David Keplinger speak of.

So, take the time to enjoy the connection poetry creates while you read. I hope you find yourself aware of what makes life so precious.

PART 1:

FALLING LEAVES

Ghosts tugging me—
wind; pulled by those
who fell
before

Into the Orange Grove

Pacing the orange grove,
eyes sting as I trace the bones of trees.
Peels litter the path, half-heartedly half-eaten.
I take off my shoes, feel the fruit
rot between my toes.

Slim branches,
rough to touch.
More trees now than before.
More trees tomorrow than today.
I must have planted a handful of them—
no way to be sure.

The gate squeals
as oranges peel themselves,
casting off their layers to reveal
every thought I've had.

I hold one in my palm,
squeeze its juice out in my hands,
can't bear the bite: sour sweetness.

If I let you in,
you can have a piece,
but the grove belongs to me.

You look around, I know
it's so much less than you expected:
untamed and ugly.

Once the mystery is gone
so is the sweetness.
You'll never reach for me again.
A creaking, splitting noise
like floorboards being ripped out,
then a crash like a hurricane.

Your footprints sink and soak into the soil,
your axe landing with a thump.
Teeth into fruit, white needles digging,
sugar diluted by drool.

I ask you to say something,
anything. You just smile, juice
dribbling down your chin.
Don't you know you
can never return?

Crunch

A beetle crosses my path.
Blue jolly rancher,
glow of sweetness.

Shimmering glass.
Steel toe breaks the blue—
crunch.

One fissure spreads,
the entire piece
destroyed.

Leaks gray insides:
minuscule heart,
twitching fragments.

Ocean of gray grit,
signature in blue.
Cement stamped.

Maybe a spirit
leaves its
shell.

Echo of roaring
water down the drain
brown leaf bits, rust.

Tumble with
crushed carcass.
Take it from my sight.

imy2

u + i, under the covers of ur couch bed,
a rose petal atop 2 pixies.
listening 2 a song about aching,
trading half-truths,
ily drips from our lips like wine.

im under the sheets of my bed,
we fly farther from each other
our wings caught in unwanted wind.
that make it hard 2 breathe.

i text: u ok?
u text me u miss me:
ur favorite half-truth.
2 silver-skinned fairies,
handcuffed in iron
itch & burn.

tighten.
2 heart emojis & an imy
I break out in a rash,
send 2 back, roll over.

Forgiveness

Forgiveness crawled
in my skull as I slept.
Hatched eggs in my ears—
flees on thousands of tiny legs.
An infestation.

Hurricane

Try to fall asleep at night,
hurricanes behind my eyes.
Hurricane in a bone bottle—
call it insomnia.

Thoughts. Thunder between ears.
Can't sleep, haven't slept, nothing new.
Close my eyes, sleep through the storms.
Can't sleep, I miss her.

Wind defines a hurricane,
long-windedness a poet.
She was both.

She saw. Eye of a hurricane—
lost her before we knew that kind of calm.
Except for small moments:
waking up or sleeping beside a text.
Good morning, beautiful. Good night,
sweet dreams, if only.

Tempest-maker, Goddess of the Rain.
Gone before I caught my breath.
The best storm the world has seen:
name it after her.

Our poetry, misery. Interchangeable.
Texted me she loved me every day.
Inevitable destruction of it all.
Glass-blowing breath,
rests in shards now.

Her welcome back:
handfuls of lightning bolts, mouthfuls of thunder.
Her absence took something.
Houses washed ashore in wreckage,
the ocean took a bite of the world.

Roofs ripped clean off, faces
stolen to reveal skulls underneath.
Home upon home wiped away like
unwanted sentences.

Trees stripped bone bare,
skinned of their greenery.
Should have just forgiven.
Could have slept easier.

Rain subsides. Wet sand. Sink together.
Leave again. This time let her go.
Hear from her less than hurricanes—
my paradox, my hurricane.

When she can't sleep, does she think of me?

Scent of Sincerity

Her house
was alive:
halls smelled
like lavender,
bedrooms
crushed pine.

Her voice grew
leaves,
pink buds
their scent, a smile—
lingers long
after

the tomatoes
on the windowsill
make howling
faces

long after
the for-sale sign
goes up,
just as the lilacs
are severed
below the
bloom.

Venus Flytrap

Teeth, hair-thin swords.
Mouth a clam.

No pearl, no fortune.
Hollow throat, cavern

goes to the ground.
Sweat pimples, clear welts

condensation
on her cheeks.

Opened book, no words
story of hunger, taste.

Waiting to swallow
wriggling gnats.

Winged olives.
Tasteful black.

Still living, locked
away, unwanted secret.

Jack Frost

Snow globe eyes, polar smile.
Now, though, snow doesn't appear
as angel tears.
But sits at the bottom,
eggs rotting.
Stuck, like me.

Snow used to arabesque
behind his eyes.
Two blizzards now plowed apart—
I remember the winter words.

My breath white smoke
each time we spoke.
Soon my eyes and teeth chattered.
Shattering the rapture
of the frost-nibbled time spent.

Frost on phone screens,
trash the fractal fractured glass.
All seasons pass.

My Open Relationship

getting dark,
He stares out
the window again.
i'm facing the wall,
can't look at each other.
too deep in the coffin
to breathe.

i say talk, because i'm talking
too loud. remember me.
speak, you vampire, or at least look
at me, cry, scream, or screw me
right here on this floor.

made fire soft in my palms. For me.
let me taste His ashes in my mouth
like He was forever. the fire
grew dimmer daily. i wanted warmth,
He needed quiet.

suitcase packed, unfolded clothes.
don't ask where, why, when. gone.
there were days He carried the sun
in His hands, now it sets
on its own.

apartment empty for months.
in my dreams He opens the windows,
tells me to jump. i always do.
at midnight, i tell the space
He took up i love you three times.

don't mean it even once.
He left while the sun rose,
cutting each shadow into an arc.
some nights i think
about the stake
embedded in His heart

taken from His hand.
the sun, too much for this world.

Green Jacket

You spilled beer on my green jacket.
I still have it, stain and all.

You leave cavities behind
eating away at bone, insatiable carnivore.

I smile through the scent,
pink blood shimmers on your neck.

I can't breathe your tainted air
you dip the world in frosting gone stale.

I wear my green jacket, you take me
into the sweetness of your pit stains.

Your voice rolls out,
watered down syrup.

"I still love you," you say, drunk
on your own tongue.

Never Get Better

Found a get well card
in the back
of my drawer.

Behind broken crayons,
and a container with three
orange Tic Tacs left.

The card, made
when I missed you.

Colors on white paper,
dark enough to know
how hard I pressed.

Pink crayon heart
drawn, wobbled lines,
but with care.

The card never saw your
fractured green eyes.

Only the inside of
my palms as I
tore it up.

Resting
in pieces
in a trashcan.

Desire

Princess, glass crown.
Lets me dress her, comb her
hair that spirals downward
tangles of night sky,
eyes even darker.

She tells me the enemy
has a kingdom that
will be hers, all she needs—
one night alone with the prince.
Horns behind her ears.

She plots while she bathes.
Likes when I draw her bath,
only silver fairy blood will do.
Talks about bodies;
I never mind listening.

I tell her I'd kneel even
if she wasn't my dictator.
She laughs, a screaming wind,
splintered emerald embers in her eyes.
I hardly remember anything else

besides the end of the night, her
stepping into a silver silk nightgown,
smiling with two rows of teeth—
her eyes jaded jade, they say
try me.

Apothecary

Clear plastic, black pills.
Knots of weariness.
Glass skin wrapped around drops.
Ride to him in the night,
carriage drawn by headless horses,
hooves fall like beating hearts.
I forgot what that sounded like after
I died three years ago.

Push my nail into a pill,
oozing purple venom.
It's impossible for him
to lose all of the pills I offered.
So much more than medicine:
My bones grind under his molars.
My blood in the color when it dissolves,
salt smile that lasts a lifetime.

Called myself an apothecary,
always had antidotes.
They worked on him,
he doesn't call anymore.
Used to keep a stock to satisfy:
vial on every surface, in every bag.
But I gave him everything.
Now when I need a cure:
nothing left.

Deadly

The curse clings like rust.
I'm caught in the clutches
of sweet diseases I love.

Anarchy is a taste in my mouth—
prickers plucked from the ground.
Maybe I'll stop digesting dirt
when I say the three words
that aren't *you are sickness.*

Obsession is a reason to mourn
a heart is a sickness
we should be grateful for.

Pop

Bubbles
strike the surface of the soda.
Hands reaching for lifeguards
that will never come.

Drink
from the cup. Let the buoyant
air taste my tongue, lips made
for lies not love.

Never
did I believe you.
Digesting sugar until
stomachaches shipwrecked.

Lips
kiss the rim. Bubbles collect.
Gaps I'll never fill. I strike
the surface until it kills.

[Save as Draft]

[Typing] . . .
Message Deleted.

Friendship: [Save as Draft].
Waiting . . .

Where are you?
Refusal to communicate: [Save as Draft].

The Idea of Who You Could Be: *Favorited*
Read again. Again. Again. Can't

. . . delete all in inbox?

Smoke rising from a smile so familiar it aches.
Purple rivers run behind blighted eyes.

I type out letters for you, saying I prayed for your
happiness more than my own.

[Deleting . . .]
Clearing out the trash.

That takes time.
Do you want to Uninstall?

Are you sure? Yes.
Regret: [Save as Draft].

Witch Doctor

Her shark smile could restart
my heart if I had one.
Someone else removed it a couple
hundred times, forgot where they left it.

She likes to cut me open every few hours,
centerpiece never on display.
Veins dripping with longing for meaning.
She ties knots to stop the bleeding.
Turns my organs over in her palms,
puts them back wrong.
I'd call her a witch doctor,
but there is no cure.

Dragon's blood in the first potion.
My insides to embers, she bathes me
in frostbite to save my life.
Second round, tried her favorite—
antidote so insidious even she doesn't laugh,
poured down my throat—
black fungus molting in my lungs.

To bring me back, injects me with fire ants.
Crawl in my veins, sizzling blood to sand.
She says:
Taste venom on my lips, infecting
through sweat on my skin.
Let me keep your heart
in one of my jars, a poison to adore.

crop circles

i create crop circles
traced by my shadow—
their pattern forgotten
in the dark.

saunter to nowhere,
that's my favorite.
solitude is my affair.
shed glasses, impaired.

trudge on a sidewalk,
streetlights glowing bones.
only destination:
somewhere alone.

car sweeps by
with yellow headlights
on its way to a hometown
no one knows.

talking, sighing,
heeding a heart rush.
it's easy to speak
when they're not beside us.

tell the ghosts that follow
don't say a word.
they say they miss me,
but they are liars.

the breath i breathe:
forged hot in hell.
the best silences
can be felt

i walk to worship words
that make me ill
and the world
when it is still.

PART 2:

BARK IN KNOTS

Through turbulent
nights—twisting
myself in
knots
only I can

untie.

Dragon Bones

i lie among my dragon bones,
gnawing on the jagged edges
until the carcass is picked clean,
but i keep digging among the ribs.

friends come to my cave.
eyes widen, tell me to stop,
but their voices are so quiet
like ash scratching cobblestones.

i pass along a shard of femur
or a knotted vein,
gifts dripping with color,
the entrails of my lavender madness;
i'm told their smell is sweet.

my heart detaches with a click,
sliding from its keep.
but i remain alive, ready to show
pale scales under eyes
and fingernails.

friends are not willing to blame me.
not even after i smile widely
with shreds of diaphragm
between my teeth.

enter my lair with a quiet question:
"if i may ask, how do you do this?"
but that is between
the bones and me.

Ogre Appetite

Goblins collect. Hoard.
Their greed, insatiable.
But so is mine.

Peanut butter on a spoon.
Sugar and honey.
Come running. Traps click shut.
Locking them in.

Their faces peel away
like orange rinds.
Goblins taste just like chicken.

As I lie awake I imagine
them clawing their way
through my organs.

I worry I will cough up
skulls in my sleep,
or worse,
that one night

young goblins will hatch
inside me and crawl
through my teeth
out onto my bed.

That I'll wake up
Surrounded
by the children
of my appetite.

Werewolf

I hold my breath
under covers.
Hold heat in my body.
A wolf will enter.

The pack run into
the wall so quickly:
One stops, then two.
Here, wolves find me.

One, cadaverous,
will sniff the air.
Heart rush:
it knows I am there.

Grow claws of my own
in hallowed sleep.
Soon they will find
a new fiend.

solitary

palm against cheek

fingers against hair

knuckles against pillow.

onyx ocean choking on

what's left of a lighthouse

solitary knight, no sword.

my thumb tucked

behind my ear—

a comfort,

someone is there.

Caught

in the shadow of a
gargoyle
leathery ligaments of
stone
walk faster
soon as i think
it might catch me
it has
Catch my breath in a cage
Catch myself: remade
Catch a cataclysm to crave
When my heart is heaviest
I climb out of the grave
Now I can breathe
Catch air, catch light
hold it like a
whisper inside

Stinging Tears

In public.
No energy.
Can't run
to the bathroom
to hide.

Timer goes off. Five
minutes pass.
Swipe snot with the
sleeve of my sweater.
Freeze myself.

I am Medusa
turned to stone with
only my reflection.
Make me the monster
I am.

hru

sending a txt // can't
bring myself // 2 ask for it
how r u // good u
small tears squeeze // out
run // down my nose
my eyes // ugly // in the mirror
maybe i'll send an idk // glad
no 1 can see me cry // glad
u can't see me
thru the screen // can't send //

ignore // answer tomorrow
when im // better

for the heads i cut

4am: hydra of mine
life hitting left & right
behind on work
frantically fight
forget to breathe
overloading me

sorry i went for the head first
only makes the madness worse

Medusa

Her name doesn't matter.
She was a woman.
She was nothing
but a wine glass drained of red
on the drying rack.
They gave her a weapon
then cadavered her for using it.
Left her headless
with no grave.
The gods are no crueler than we are.
They used her even dead.

Mother

I want to say
I took a step back today.

Reborn Earth   inside me,
Can't speak through the ivy.

She hears me wash the goblet,
Calls my name, can't stop it.

I'm   distracted and unheard
Can't hear her words.

Glass goblet, delicate,
Wine is not the only red drip.

Call Off the Operation

Scissors too
familiar. Surgeon from
somewhere, doesn't matter.
He has a beard that's brittle
straw tickling my neck.
Cut me open down the middle
like a child dissecting a teddy bear
pull the stuffing out from
a jagged line.

I say he's cut too deep.
He says save all complaints for
after the operation. Sewn up
with our best thread, serrated
starlight. Can't even tell him:
I can't breathe. Can't breathe.
First he replaces all my
organs: elastic heart,
like spiderwebs in a knot.

Throat a gun barrel, lungs
two napkins wrapping up
leftovers. Filled with
air, enough to last a lifetime.
All my bones are intertwined with hungry
steel, will grow and replace all imperfections.
I'll be a tin man, unable to miss a note.
Can I make a request? leave my skin,
I don't want to be plastic.

We haven't even gotten to your brain yet—

New electricity I can recharge any
day, new wires to cross so I never
implode, never cry at night, never fail to see
the bigger picture through plaster
eyes that won't allow tears to fall.
No, leave my eyes, I like
the blue. Don't need stronger sight.
Leave one piece alone,
even if it's one little finger.

Sold every inch of me for better
parts, so that blue disease
will never terrorize
me again. Didn't realize how
much I loved needing glasses to see
needing someone to hold my hand.
Didn't love the fractures in my life
until he replaced my bones with steel.
I never broke a bone and now I never will.

Rumpelstiltskin

Straw. Grasp, come away with a tickle of gold
Grab handfuls, come away with a whisper.
Tears, diamonds from your palace.
Gather, gather, gone.

Yellow like corn, brittle dead hairs
from the ground,
now everything is made of it.
But soon it will all shine like moonlight.

First I trade my smile, pearl necklace
then I trade my eyes, rings from fingers.
I, your scarecrow, made from you.
Would rather break than give you what you
now ask for in exchange.

I gave you everything
to save my neck,
but now you want hers.
The one I've created from my flesh.
Carved out of my soul, she is not for sale.

Leave with hunger, howl that haunts.
Spin it all, come away anew.
You say I'll never guess your name
never own you,

but I saw you last night singing
yourself to sleep.
You gave away a secret;
I swallowed it for keeps.

To the Boy Muttering

to his tangled self
outside the library.

a page that never got unfolded.
someone tried to mark their place
and never went back.

prismatic nonsense
needed to be spoken aloud.
paperclip bent out of shape.

eyes two marbles rolling in circles
mind in swirling painted whorls
like the sea mixing with the sunset
who knows where the water ends
and sky begins.

I've seen you before.

I knew your sorrow
before I knew you.

The Last Supper

My grandmother reimagined the painting.
Her own crafted swarm of holy people.
I loved the story of Judas,
someone with some sense.

When she painted it she touched up
God's left hand—
most people wouldn't notice.
I am looking for the mistake.

Maybe the paint's
too thin, or the fingers too slim.
looking at my own
fingers; wait.

The painting reminds me
of when my skin was see-through.
When my mind
was feasting on itself.

I was God for about a week,
cost me ten pounds and
liquified my atheism
so I could drink it—it's white.

Pearl drops for Christ's eyes,
too famous to be forgotten.
Even in my house,
even in my head,

long after my throat
is dry.

Leonardo

The best part of beauty is the haze.
Yellow dimness like a single lightbulb
hanging in a cement basement
and there in the center: a woman.

A woman without jewelry or makeup
or other ornaments of youth
we take for granted.

Her only loveliness is her laughter
at the jester nearby : not amusement
from the way the light hates us.

Stage lights show us the way
the corners of our smiles wrinkle
with the words we have unleashed.
Never stand in that lighting.
Dim lights show the truth;
She rules the shadows, bruises
on a fruit she blessed
with a teeth kiss.

House by the Sea

Crash   on the shore
Crash   in my mind
Can't tell which waves are
keeping me up

I wonder if I would give up
Half the waves in my brain
   extraordinary ones
to find life easier

I am content
but it's happiness on a cliff
above an unholy sea
or a glass plate teetering on the corner
of the countertop

Crash   on the tile
Crash   in my head
There are no acid waves
Just ordinary waves
ordinary for me

Deadly for me
What can I do
but breathe?
And let them
haunt   my
dreams

Persephone

I invaded her garden where pomegranates grew.
Rubies glittering in stolen moonlight.

The limbs of her trees looked
like arms of a sick child.

She was starving so I crept in every night
to water the roots, to bring her back to life.

One night she caught me in her orchard.
Said she could heal on her own.

That she was a witch doctor with her own ways
of finding life in her glow.

She cast a curse on me to never grow
a tree like hers.

Blood would be the only red
ever held in my hands.

As I fled her garden for the last time, I took a handful
of her seeds and planted them in my own orchard.

But the saplings sprouted shriveled
like corpses left to rot.

Palace at Night

Take you to my palace of trees.
Where I grow shadow fire that
makes your eyes turn inside out
and roll down your throat—

We hide scars under leaves.
from swallowing lightning.
Can't be washed off.
Covered by scabs of skin,
colorful smiles, butchered laughter.

See mud on your shoes
From walking at night when
I'm not by your side.
Rain prickles
in the back of our minds.
The sky tastes sickening.

You ask if the trees
made me contort that way.
You think you know
what you can't; even if
you've seen every forest,
you've never walked in
mine.

PART 3:

SPROUTING ROOTS

Spreading like sunlight;
growing the most when
I realize
    I'm never
        truly
   alone

Nuclear

Ash or snow, toxic bits flutter down.
landing and making a film on my brain.

Fresh layer of skin, ashen.
separates thoughts from eyelids.

Reach through--- I say, empty
I'm trying--- you cry in the breeze

I dig my hands in the ash until my fingertips are singed.
put my bare feet in until they itch.

There's a screen between the wreckage
and the haven that housed me when the bomb razed.

Can you pull the screen away?
I cut a hole and stretch a hand through its face.

it scratches red pen lines, signs the snakes in my wrist
gathers embers under the surface of my flesh.

your hand is in mine despite what stands between us
someday we'll be free, but for now it's enough.

In the Underworld

I met a mirror
a frozen ocean,
constellation scene:
who I used to be.

The waves black roses
rolling, laughing sorrow.
The day will come when I break
the surface of this world's horror.

I can imagine
coming up for air like a
monster from the sea.
For years I've dwelt beneath.
Now it's time to be the beast.

Today I tell the mirror
the stars are rearranging for me;
I'll discard black petal winters
shed coats of apathy.

Watery fear runs down.
I rise and hurricanes
cry in my wake.
Time to show—
I've changed.

Spoon

Collecting dust in its basin
particles floating on water
like a shipwreck.

Or the beads of a
necklace, maybe
a rosary.

droplets of
a rusting sink, like red
tinged eyes.

Now the utensil submerges
in water too cold
to drink:

from underground
where spirits who live there
forget where they came from.

Hand mirror without glass
turns the face upside down
because that's the way it belongs.

Cupped hands colliding,
reminding us we're
never quite right.

Sister Lark

I found you in every folded down
corner of my diary
yes, the pages are yellowed
isn't that beautiful?

crinkled sails with letters
in the language of 3am
messages, send? not yet
tell you I love you I love
your softened corners
from all the times
I've flipped back to reread.

when I was a kid you'd sing
and I'd listen through the wall
my heartbeat the rhythm
of home's symphony.

you remember everything I forget
the end of my sentences
the wings of larks
stirring in your heart.

you want to fly North,
I dream of southern skies.
the songbirds we raised together
are meant to take flight.

but my diary never runs out of pages.
I'll write, no matter we're apart.
call when you fly my way,
I'll hear the song, wherever you are.

Box of Turtles

the gift wasn't wrapped,
but your smile was the rosiest
bow that could top it off.

a gift from a woman I never met
given through your hands.
bark intertwined in glowing patterns.

inside the box she gave:
two turtles.

the plastic turtle stands with wide eyes
behind thick-rimmed glasses.
he gives me a faded smile
that tells me not to worry.

another is ceramic,
dark patterns on his shell.
he swims in the box with hollow flippers.
I wish him good morning.

their shells tell stories of green rivers,
tossing and turning in swirls.

their faces smile like green cherubs
who learn that heaven
can be a wicker box.

she was an old friend,

I'm young enough to love
the turtles like they were always mine.
A gift from a ghost, still alive inside.

Cigarettes & Saints

Yes, I see. I tell Mary.
The pews in wooden prayer,
the wooden people hold
hope for salvation.

She knows, I'll kneel.
I am the tile floor, can't feel
the ground heated
by hell, no such luck.

Icy granite floor through
the knees of my jeans:
always tatter where
they are needed most.

Windows of the church,
light catches the crystals' hurt.
Who are the saints
crying in color?

Yellow and red coalesce,
overcome me, climb higher
submission of the forest
to the fire.

Questions, confessions,
hot pokers to the soul.
Denim to shreds and cold tile
mouth to ashes, taste of carelessness.

Needles set afire, wreckaged.
My forest fire ravages,
tearing apart the saplings I know.
Cataclysms need time to grow.

Orange anger, daggered fingers,
gorging on green until
there's nothing
but silt rivers.

New sprouts from the ashes,
new colors in the glasses.
She tells me I will learn
from the burning.

Sleeping Venus

I forgive you, but don't ever paint my portrait.
My eyeballs roll around behind thin
curtained lids: I see dresses.
They soak me like syrup, so sweet—
my tongue and eyes weep.

One dress, lace so fragile,
eggshells with which I dare not graze
the ground.

"Try me on" the dress aches.
"Be curved in all the right places.
Be icing, never more than frosting."

I mold into another dress and another
gown like a liquid I can't get off.

We paint Venus naked. We always do.
Maybe she will rage when she wakes
to finds painters carving her
curves into their canvases.

I can identify my spine
in the mirror when it glows,
but to you, who holds the brush
and the eyes in chalk hands,
what do you know?

Michelangelo Painting the Sistine Ceiling

I lean backwards to create; to craft a layer of life.
Hot pins under my skin dart around inside me as I reach
again, adding a hair to a beard---a cloud puff pulled
straight.

Noah is first: a story of life told backwards through paint---
I bend backwards through pain. Speak to Noah. Him
alone.
The only one who understands.

He sees the storm to come; black fog in the eyes, mind,
ears.
Cumulating cumulonimbus created for us. Maybe I can
stop it.
Purple water line in the clouds, says chain the angels
of war.

Ocean of orange devil waves engulf all but the ark, made
more noble
than the face of Christ. Dot of gray, a nail holding the
wooden world together,
a nail holding flesh to light and light to salvation.

Can I change anything? Noah did. His hands held calluses
and deliverance.
Mine wear paint like an extra skin. I'll never shed my
sunbeams.
Even when the typhoon hurls me to the ground, breaks
my back.

I won't stop. My brush makes heaven come down.
God stays on the ceiling; I think he too loves
the taste of Earth.

A Dream I Had

My old bedroom:
the carpet, rugged pink and red,
like cheeks rubbed raw—
I let it gnaw on me.

Sleeping bag melts into chrysalis—
will I grow wings and wake with buds
growing from my back?
The hairbrush drips
from being used after a shower—

I knock
over a jar of beads.
I rock a world in between.
They scatter, bees released from a shattered hive
all different colors, a city of lives,
rolling like dyed dice—
the gamble is rigged for none,
I'll never guess the right one.

Beads fall through the carpet's scalp
into drains into ears into hands that can't help.
But I've found my fingers underwater.
I squeeze hope in fists, releasing words.
I wake up standing on the pain.
Beside me, a voice calls my name.

The Well

Fills with rain,
a mouth, drooling
over stone lips.

Trees reflect on the surface,
leaves laugh in the breeze.
Green half-devils writhe for me.
They aren't easy to name.

The rain stops.
Today the trees are thirty percent devil.
Roots gulp air; tomorrow,
seventy percent. They will swallow rain
for the droughts to come---
it is approaching, as it always does.
Likeliness of rain drops to two percent.
Roots out of Gaea's skull,
like claws scraping dirt, cursing the clouds.
Another day they will make a cross,
pray for forgiveness and rain
like the rest of us.

One day the well will close like a mouth
guiding a secret back behind
its teeth with its tongue.

Cloud Garden

Where white roses bloom like cotton
and wind aches in my lungs.
I'm in cloud cuffs, like feathers
from pillows in ringlet puffs.

The worms' faces are like the foam
at the mouths of rabid raccoons.
you can't find a face
like that on the moon.

I visit the garden
from time to time,
dance in my
marshmallow meadow.

Gates lead into garden:
blue arrow like the divide
between white on
paper with lines.

A gap in the sky where
my cloud garden
waits for when I
decide to stay.

Stranger on a Plane

She's seen cactus flowers
blooming purple mouths
I see them in her eyes
They open to catch the rain
hitting our window

She's seen sandstorms
like tunnels without centers
knots in the wind too big
to be untangled
I see them in her hands
wrinkled and ready to grab
life and tear into pieces

She hunts rattlesnakes,
says the smallest ones
are the most lethal
I know they are her in veins
only venomous when she bites
holding all of the world's
beasts in her smile

She names monsoons
like they are her sisters
thanks them for their devastation
I hear them in her voice
the echo of a fated storm

She speaks with a smile,
"Here comes the lightning."

Ode to My Gaea

I tell God pearls are not made from sand
they are made with her hands
between her fingertips

Like how she separated the sky
from the Earth with a fingernail's smile
and made gods and titans escape
from her own skin like clay

Her voice rides the waves
like crystal seafoam
when she tells stories at the
bottom of the ocean

She crafts her pearls, a sculptor
never rolling too much sand, or sea
she cries rose petals and tells me

Red is always saved for last
she reaches through thorns to save me
breathing salt water from my lungs
rebuilding the world in a rosebud

The Grove

Branches dripping
memories. Wish I could resist.

Try to grab what I can;
wake up empty handed.

Candied smell: starving but nauseating.
Never enough until we blister our taste buds.

Sit under a trunk, wonder why no other plant
will grow under my care. Why can't other seasons stay?

Want to stop eating the same fruit. Want treacle that
isn't tainted.
Stinging that doesn't linger so long. So I trim.

Beheading branches before they sprout flowers.
I pull white petals that cry out like children.

Toss them aside. Enough of sour-sweet smiles.
Oranges round and rolling in my head.

Look back at what I've done. Hundreds of trees
stripped bare, to return stronger.

Like shaving a scalp; the hair will
come back thicker.

Hide the peels and crops that no longer have use.
Like burying the naughtiness of good children.

Submerge both hands into soil.
Hold the strongest roots in my hands.

Goddess of the Rain

When I turned eleven
I planted an orange seed,
brought water in my palms:
a mirror I didn't mind looking in.
Poured my reflection onto the seed
until the oxygen in my head was clean.

Fourteen, sapling dried up.
Despite the drought
draining my soil, let her
into my grove, she brought rain,
a gentle mist, to this day
I can still bring life back
with the memory.

Sixteen when I lost her
the storm collapsed my lungs
in the forest I had grown for her
trees tipped over like drunks,
slamming into the ground,
making canyons I could never
dream of resurrecting.

Wind took her, it takes every spirit.
goddesses belong in the clouds.
Couldn't understand.
She was gone. Gathered
storms in my fists,
stirred a hurricane in my chest.

To hell with all the trees I planted.
Uprooted them, threads in a shirt
I'd been wearing too long.

So I let the rain pour like tears.
Filled the canyons with water.
Built a city, rivers as my streets,
new saplings, homes
for the life that remained.

Planted a tree in her memory,
shaped it with my hands and
trimmed it tight so it would
never grow too tall.
A bonsai, dwarfed in youth.
When I turned nineteen,
I let it grow on its own.

Jack Frost's Winter

He came to stay,
sitting in my branches
flicking off bark
with his thumb.

Didn't like the sweetness
of my fruit, said let the sour
spread, a blight only I could bring.
Froze my fruit, every bite
a cold crunch.

Some days I couldn't
find my sugar without his smile.
On days he'd leave I'd uproot
my trees like pulling out stitches.

One day Jack arrived,
ice fangs glittering in
the waning sunlight.
I said I'd give him anything.

He laughed in my face,
left with a gust of wind.
Cradled in crystal, I froze---
roots found me.

Swaddled in wood
I found warmth in the arms
of a willow tree forgotten;
I thawed.

Willow

periwinkle branches reach out to me,
the way winter falls on her each year
makes the summer nothing but a sigh.

can you believe we are so lucky?

she grew in the garden when
I was born, and I have forgotten to tell
her she is my favorite.

stand under her in fevers
wraps me in leaves
when my skeleton shivers.

asks why a blight
consumes my orange grove
each summer

asks me why people
don't stay longer.
I tell her people

show for the fruit.
she reminds me beauty is
found in the roots.

Grace

I used to chew fire trying to fall asleep
Then I met a reflection in a dream

In her eyes, lilies sway in a breeze
Her fire fades and rebirths green

Silt stirs, a cocktail of gray
Close my eyes and grow a new face

I find warmth now instead of flames.
I walk, ashes behind me: telling the story of Grace.

Bonsai

The leaves of Dad's bonsai turned brown and fell,
dirty tears on moss. He didn't stop
trimming leaves even when they dwindled
and clung to toothpick branches.

The centerpiece to the kitchen,
an ancient child dwarfed by tenderness.
The bonsai is moved and pruned and remade.
He brings it inside, outside, or

turns it on an angle, puts it on
a windowsill, gives it new sunlight.
Still it drips age and leaves.
He never stops trimming.

Ask why he cuts and cares
but then I stop wondering
when it blooms a green face
with round cheeks and eyes

brilliant enough to bring the sun
back to its sill.

ACKNOWLEDGEMENTS

I'd like to acknowledge the people who supported this book:

Joy Kidd, Marie Elena Hasson, Robert and Linda Cole, Linda Hasson, Jerrold Hellman, Eric Koester, Tia Hudson, Noah Tennant, Willow Hasson, Olivia du Pont, Gabrielle Audu, Vy-Anh Nguyen, Jackie Lamb, Rick Kidd, Annie Caroline Przypyzny, Hunter Albright, Shelby Rose and Katie Meyerson, Tina Papa, Barbara Mattera, John Hasson, Melonie Pernice, Jackson Yoder, Curtis Hayashi, Daren Roa, Chris Utz, Wayne Radziminski, Katrina Freeman, Annapurna Poduri, Lora Palazzolo, Elliana Barbuto, Haley Newlin, Rebecca Flaherty, Marisa Lemma, Joseph Chromicz, Angel Tarsatana, RJ Palmer, Kayla Gillespie, Sophie Gilbert, Julia Smith, Asher Grinberg, Travis Thomas, Cass Lauer, Peter Stevens, and Esther Phillip.

I'd also like to gratefully acknowledge David Keplinger and Bailey Blumenstock, who believed in this book from the beginning.

And an extra thank you to all the people who made this book possible. To all the friends who read my poetry, family members who supported me, and those who believed in my dream and my journey.

Made in the USA
Middletown, DE
24 August 2020

15998205R00056